117674 D0095679

j
BIO

Stewart, Mar'
Bernie Will
Leader

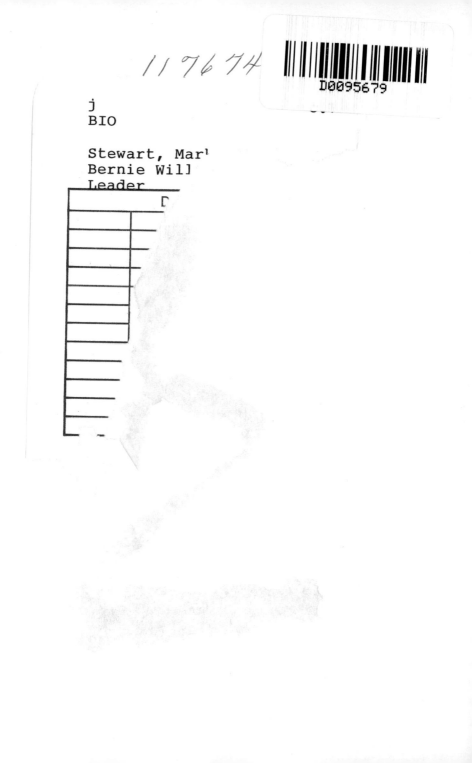

★ SPORTS STARS ★

BERNIE WILLIAMS
QUIET LEADER

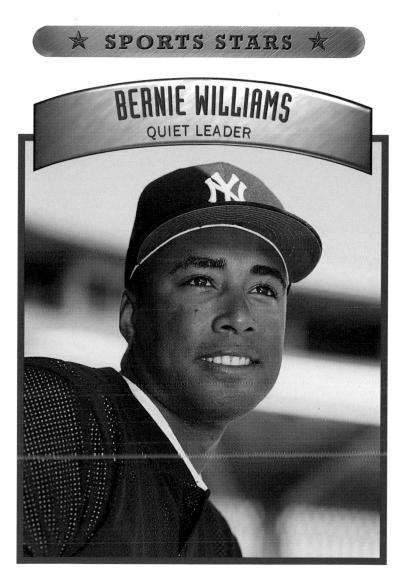

BY MARK STEWART

Children's Press®
A Division of Grolier Publishing
New York London Hong Kong Sydney
Danbury, Connecticut

Photo Credits
©: Allsport USA: 35 top, 37, 45 left (Al Bello), 39 (Stephen Dunn), 40 (Doug Pensinger); AP/Wide World Photos: 35 bottom (Dallas Morning News), 14 (Tony Esparza), 29 (Barry Jarvinen), 25 (Pat Sullivan); Barbara Jean Germano: 19 right, 44 right; Daily News, L.P.: 37 (Harry Hamburg); International Stock Photo: 9 (Andre Jenny); John Klein: 17, 21, 27, 43, 44 left, 45 right, 47; SportsChrome East/West: 26 (Jeff Carlick), cover, 22, 28, 31, 42 (Rob Tringali, Jr.), 6 (Michael Zito); Steve Crandall & Assoc. Photography: 3, 19 left, 32, 38, 41, 46; UPI/Corbis-Bettmann: 11, 13.

Visit Children's Press on the Internet at:
http://publishing.grolier.com

Library of Congress Cataloging-in-Publication Data

Stewart, Mark.
    Bernie Williams: quiet leader / by Mark Stewart.
        p. cm. — (Sports stars)
        Summary: Follows the career path of Bernie Williams, who emerged as a Yankee star in the 1996 playoffs.
        ISBN: 0-516-20968-X (lib. bdg.)   0-516-26421-4 (pbk.)
        1. Williams, Bernie, 1968– —Juvenile literature. 2. Baseball players—United States—Biography—Juvenile literature. 3. New York Yankees (Baseball team)—Juvenile literature. [1. Williams, Bernie, 1968– .
    2. Baseball players. 3. Puerto Ricans—Biography.] I. Title. II. Series.
GV865.W48S74   1998
796.357'092—dc21
[B]   97-32104
                                                               CIP
                                                               AC

CONTENTS ✶

✶

★ 1 ★

POWER SWITCH-HITTER

Bernie Williams strides confidently to home plate while one of the American League's toughest relievers completes his warm-up tosses. Bernie has already stroked two hits left-handed, but because the new pitcher is a lefty, he steps into the right-handed batter's box. Bernie eyes a couple of sliders that just miss the plate, letting each go by. Now he has the pitcher right where he wants him. The next delivery is a well-placed fastball about knee-high. But with Bernie in the box, the placement is not good enough. He strides into the pitch and snaps his bat at the ball, driving it toward the left-field stands with a loud crack. The pitcher does not even bother to look. When Bernie hits one like that, everybody in the stadium knows it is gone.

★ 2 ★

ISLAND LIFE

When you live on an island, there are two ways of looking at life. You can peer out across the water and wonder what you are missing, or you can explore the world around you. Bernabe Williams never thought much about what lay beyond the horizon when he was growing up on the Caribbean island of Puerto Rico. The boy everyone called "Bernie" was too busy with all the opportunities and adventures right in his own backyard. His parents, Rufina and Bernie, Sr., encouraged Bernie and his younger brother, Hiram, to experiment with many activities and to pursue different interests. The boys participated in

San Juan is a beautiful old city on the coast of Puerto Rico where Bernie was born and raised.

sports, played music, and learned as much as they could about the world around them.

By the age of eight, Bernie could strum many songs on the guitar. His favorite was a Puerto Rican folk song called "Verde Luz," which means "Green Light" and describes Puerto Rico's beaches and mountains. It was also at this time that Bernie first became interested in baseball.

Baseball is the most popular sport in Puerto Rico. Because of the warm weather, it is played all year long. Bernie did not understand the rules at first, but his father was willing to teach him the game. It helped that he was the fastest kid in the neighborhood. Bernie remembers his first time playing: "I could run fast, but I couldn't play. For three or four years, every day after school, my dad would teach me how to hit, throw, and run the bases."

Bernie played as often as possible. When there were not enough children to field two teams, he played stickball with Hiram and other children in his neighborhood. During these games, Bernie (who is naturally right-handed) tried batting left-handed, just like fellow Puerto Ricans Jose Cruz and Willie Montanez, who were two of the finest hitters in the major leagues. Bernie's early experiment in switch-hitting would give him a big advantage a few years later.

Houston Astro outfielder, Jose Cruz, who Bernie says
inspired him to try batting from the left side

Tall and thin, Bernie was not much of a power threat. During games he would try to hit the ball on the ground and then use his blazing speed to reach first base safely. This was enough, however, to earn him a regular spot on some very good teams. He found himself playing in Puerto Rico's top youth leagues against future major-league stars such as Ivan Rodriguez and Juan Gonzalez.

Bernie was also becoming a big baseball fan. The New York Yankees were very popular in San Juan during the late 1970s, and the successes of the team's Puerto Rican pitcher, Ed Figueroa, were followed very closely by adults and children. Bernie liked Figueroa, but he was far more interested in the Yankee hitters. "I used to watch Reggie Jackson, Chris Chambliss, Willie Randolph, Mickey Rivers, Bucky Dent, and Graig Nettles," he says, adding that he dreamed about wearing the Yankee pinstripes someday.

Slugger Reggie Jackson hits one of his 563 career home runs. Jackson's achievements made Bernie want to be a Yankee someday.

Bernie's future, however, appeared to be in another area. His musical abilities earned him a scholarship to the Escuela Libre de Musica, a school for gifted young musicians. He enrolled at the age of 13 and had the time of his life. Like students in other schools, Bernie and his classmates took subjects such as math, history, and science. But the rest of the day was spent studying, composing, and playing music.

Bernie's passion for music is still equal to his passion for baseball.

During free periods and after school, Bernie and his friends would search the hallways looking for a spot that produced the best sound, then launch into a long jam session. Over the next few years, he learned how to play everything from classical music to jazz to heavy metal.

Outside of school, Bernie continued playing baseball and competing in other sports. Finally, at the age of 17, he was forced to make a choice. When a baseball player reaches his 17th birthday, he can be signed by a major-league organization. During the summer of 1985, while Bernie was still 16, a scout from the New York Yankees watched him play. He was so sure Bernie would be a star that he urged the club to "hide" him from other teams until he turned 17. In a clever maneuver, the Yankees paid for Bernie to attend a special baseball camp in Connecticut. There they could evaluate his talent more closely and, more importantly, keep other teams from scouting him. The Yankees liked what they saw, and that September, on Bernie's 17th birthday, they offered him a contract.

★ 3 ★

COMING TO AMERICA

Bernie Williams knew that becoming a
professional baseball player meant putting
aside his musical career. It also meant that
he would not receive a scholarship from the
University of Puerto Rico, where he considered
studying to become a doctor. His parents told
him that he could always go to college later if
baseball did not work out. And he could always
return to his music, too. Baseball, they all agreed,
is something you can do only when you are very
young. "It was a hard choice," says Bernie.
"At that time, what are the odds of making
it to the big leagues? Not good. Making it as
a musician would have probably been harder.

Bernie collects his thoughts between pitches. He began switch-hitting while playing with AA Albany in 1989.

The safest thing was to go to college and get a degree, but I chose this. When my career is over, I'll probably want to do something in the field of medicine. But right now, it's baseball."

The following spring, Bernie joined the Sarasota Yankees. Playing with and against other young prospects, he distinguished himself as the top base runner in the Gulf Coast League. Bernie stole 33 bases in just 61 games, and he led the league with 45 runs scored. He played well in the outfield, too, making more putouts than anyone at his position and committing just three errors.

In 1988, at the age of 19, Bernie was the Carolina League batting champion with an average of .335. He was developing just as the Yankees had envisioned. He was becoming more patient at the plate, more aggressive on the bases, and nearly flawless in the outfield.

Prior to 1989, Bernie was putting up big numbers batting only from the right side of the plate. During spring training that year,

Bernie gets the sign from his third base coach after being promoted to AAA Columbus.

Buck Showalter, who would work with Bernie at several levels

he mentioned that he had fooled around with switch-hitting as a kid. Buck Showalter, who would later manage Bernie in the majors, suggested he step across the plate and give it a try. After just a few left-handed hacks, Showalter was convinced. He informed Bernie that he was now officially a switch-hitter!

Bernie split the 1989 season between the AA Albany/Colonie Yankees and the AAA Columbus Clippers, just one level below the majors. He began slowly but finished strong, and over the winter he believed that he had earned a real shot at a big-league job. But on the last day of spring training in 1990, the Yankees sent him back to AA. The problem was that the organization was jammed with talented outfielders. Bernie understood his demotion was not a reflection of his abilities; the Yankees simply wanted him in a place where he could play every day. Still, he was furious. "I didn't walk out or anything," he remembers, "but I contemplated quitting. I called my mom that day and told her, 'Maybe this isn't such a good idea.' But she told me to stick it out."

Bernie decided the best way to show the Yankees they had made a mistake was to play better than all of the outfielders in front of him. By the end of the 1990 season he had done just that. While New York finished dead last in the

American League's Eastern Division, Bernie led his team to the best record in the Eastern League and topped all players with 39 stolen bases, 98 walks, and 91 runs. He and his wife, Waleska, also had their first child that September. It was quite a year.

Bernie says his mother convinced him to return to Albany in 1990, where he had a tremendous year.

Bernie displays the power stroke that won him a spot on the Yankees in July 1991.

★ 4 ★

MAN IN THE MIDDLE

As the 1991 season began, only two things concerned the Yankees about Bernie Williams: his power and durability. He had grown to 6' 2", but he was still a singles hitter. Most everyone agreed that this would make him ideally suited to be a leadoff man when he reached the majors, but during his first five seasons in the organization he had suffered a series of nagging injuries. And as every fan knows, you cannot be a "table-setter" if you are slowed down by the everyday aches and pains a baseball player can expect to experience.

Bernie knew the Yankees were concerned about him, but he used their doubt as a reason to do better. "You have to take criticisms as a challenge," he believes. "I like surprising people."

Bernie put the organization's fears to rest by belting out 14 doubles, 6 triples, and 8 home runs in just half a season with the Clippers. He played all-out, and he played every day. When Yankee center fielder Roberto Kelly hurt his wrist in July, Bernie was called to New York to replace him.

In his first big-league game, Bernie got one hit and knocked in two runs against the Baltimore Orioles. He collected nine hits in his first nine games, including his first home run as a major leaguer. When Kelly was ready to play again, the Yankees told him to start learning a new position. Bernie was the team's new center fielder.

Bernie receives a high five from Coach Willie Randolph.

Bernie uses his upper body to turn on a fastball.

Bernie had his ups and downs as a rookie. During September he experienced the worst batting slump of his life. "I was thinking too much instead of just letting my ability take over," he says. Still, the Yankees were pleased with Bernie's defense and baserunning, and they especially liked the fact that he did not tighten up in pressure situations. And although Bernie had trouble with off-speed pitches, no hurler in the league could sneak a fastball past him.

★ ★ ★

By the following summer, Bernie had locked up the center field position for good. At the beginning of August, he was moved into the leadoff spot, and from August 12 to the end of the season, he reached base in 49 straight games. It was one of the few highlights in a dismal season for New York, which had a losing record for the third year in a row. The losing bothered Bernie, who took out his frustration on opponents with aggressive play in the outfield and on the bases. Many of his teammates were

Despite his calm, friendly appearance, Bernie is very competitive and emotional.

surprised at Bernie's intensity. When he first joined the team, they nicknamed him "Bambi" because he looked so gentle and innocent. "People were mistaking my shyness for weakness," Bernie says now. "You can't really see it, but I'm very emotional. I'm like a volcano."

The losing ended in 1993, when the Yankees brought in three experienced veterans: Paul O'Neill, Wade Boggs, and Jimmy Key. Also, manager Buck Showalter was not afraid to experiment with his lineup. Bernie began the year as the team's leadoff hitter, but Showalter believed that he could be a run-producer. He moved Boggs, one of history's most consistent singles hitters, to the top spot in the batting order and dropped Bernie down to sixth, where he could hit with men on base. The change worked beautifully, and the Yankees began winning. They finished in second place with a record of 88–74.

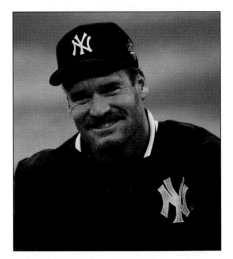

Wade Boggs, whose move into the leadoff spot gave Bernie a chance to hit in the middle of the order

Bernie times his jump perfectly as he prepares to rob
Chicago slugger Frank Thomas of a home run.

In 1994, the Yankees were in first place—and Bernie was enjoying his best year as a big leaguer—when the season ended in August because of a labor dispute. By then, he had blossomed into one of the best all-around players in the game.

Bernie began the 1995 season slowly. But during the last four months of the season, he batted over .330. In August alone he collected 46 hits. And during one week in September, Bernie carried the team on his back when he reached base 15 times in 17 at bats. He also established himself as the team's quiet leader. Bernie credits All-Star first baseman Don Mattingly for showing him how to handle this role. Mattingly, who was playing his final season in 1995, once told Bernie that the key to being a leader was to come ready to play every day. "You hear about the 'Yankee way' at a young age in the organization, but I didn't really understand it," says Bernie. "But it took only a week of watching Donnie—the way he carried himself on and off the field—to realize what being a Yankee is all about."

Yankee Don Mattingly, who taught Bernie how to be a leader

Bernie shatters his bat while swinging at a fastball.

★ 5 ★

PRESSURE PERFORMER

The Yankees finished second behind the Boston Red Sox in the Eastern Division, but they still qualified for the 1995 playoffs as the American League's wild card team. During New York's divisional series against the Seattle Mariners, baseball fans around the country saw Bernie Williams at his best. In five of the most pressure-packed games ever played, he batted .429 with eight runs scored. In Game Three, Bernie belted home runs from both sides of the plate—a first in postseason play. And whenever the team needed him to come through, he did.

Sadly for Bernie, the Yankees lost in the final inning of the final game. But he learned something important about himself: he loved the pressure of the postseason. "It's like a father waiting for his wife to deliver," Bernie, now a father of three, explains. "You get to the point where you are so focused, nothing else matters."

The Yankees cruised to the division title in 1996, with Bernie establishing himself as New York's top player. He belted 29 home runs, drove in and scored more than 100 runs, and batted over .300 for the second year in a row. Bernie could not wait for the playoffs to start. He sensed all season long that something special was happening, and he felt ready to have a huge postseason. In the first round of the division playoffs, the Yankees faced the Texas Rangers, a hard-hitting team led by a couple of old friends from the Puerto Rican youth leagues: Ivan Rodriguez and Juan Gonzalez.

Gonzalez nailed New York pitchers for five home runs in four games. But Bernie was every bit as good. He matched Gonzalez hit for hit and played spectacular defense. With the Yankees down 4–0 in Game Four, Bernie clubbed home runs from both sides of the plate again and led his team to a 6–4 victory and a series win.

Juan Gonzalez (above)
is congratulated by
teammates after one
of his five home runs.
Bernie (right) robs Texas
Ranger Rusty Greer of a
home run during Game
Three of the American
League Divisional Playoff.

Bernie watches his home run sail over the left field wall. This blast won Game Two of the 1996 ALCS against the Baltimore Orioles.

Bernie slides home safely against the Orioles in Game Three of the ALCS. His daring play gave the Yankees the boost they needed to win the pennant.

Against the Orioles in the American League Championship Series (ACLS), Bernie again spurred his team to a comeback victory, with a .474 average, 2 home runs, and 6 RBIs. In Game Three, the pivotal contest of the series, he broke Baltimore's back by racing home with the winning run when the Orioles botched a relay throw. It was the kind of heads-up baseball that Bernie had been playing all year. The Orioles, who had been beating the Yanks until then, never held a lead again. The Yankees swept the remaining two games for their first pennant in 15 seasons. No one was surprised when Bernie was named the series MVP.

"I found this great balance between being intense and relaxed," he says of his playoff performance. "And nothing could intimidate me—not the fans, not the other team, not any situation we were faced with."

Bernie receives his trophy as MVP of the 1996 ALCS.

Bernie hits a left-handed home run against the Braves in Game Three of the 1996 World Series.

That high level of confidence became contagious as the Yankees prepared to meet the Atlanta Braves in the 1996 World Series. And it is a good thing it did, for Atlanta's game plan was simple and straightforward: don't let Bernie beat us. The scheme worked, as the Braves gave him almost nothing to hit. In six games, he hit just one home run and managed a mere four hits. But Bernie's teammates picked up where he left off, stroking timely hits against one of the best pitching staffs in baseball history. After dropping the first two

The Yankees celebrate their amazing World Series victory.

games in New York, the Yankees took all three games in Atlanta, then came back to Yankee Stadium and finished off the shell-shocked Braves to become world champions. Though he batted just .167 for the series, Bernie still led the Yankees in RBIs.

Bernie finished the postseason with a .345 average, 16 RBIs, and 6 home runs— more round-trippers than anyone had ever hit in any postseason. Some fans were disappointed that he did not produce another superhuman performance during the World Series, but Bernie is quick to point out that those fans are missing the point. "I don't care if I'm a hero," he maintains. "I just want to win."

Since his unforgettable 1996 season, Bernie has been a featured attraction wherever New York has played. Fans now expect spine-tingling baseball whenever he steps on the field.

Bernie receives congratulations from his teammates.

Bernie celebrates during the World Series parade for the New York Yankees.

At the end of the 1997 season, the Yankees prepared to repeat their success from the previous year. But the fortune that had smiled upon them during the 1996 postseason deserted them in their series against the Cleveland Indians. In Game Four, the Yankees' ace reliever Mariano Rivera surrendered a game-tying home run in the eighth inning. The stunned Yankees went on to lose the series in five games. Bernie's performance was also disappointing. Although he made great defensive plays and drove in two critical runs in Game Five, Bernie did not match the success of his 1996 postseason.

★ ★ ★

"I know I haven't reached my peak," he insists. "I'm still learning every day. I definitely need to improve some things. I'm working on my mental approach. I have to improve my focus and get in the right frame of mind for every game."

That is not at all what major-league pitchers want to hear. With Bernie Williams now firmly established as one of the game's most dangerous all-around performers, they certainly do not want him getting any better.

Bernie knows the fans expect a lot from him now. He tries to improve everyday.

C ★ H ★ R ★ O ★ N

1968 • September 13: Bernie is born in San Juan, Puerto Rico.

1985 • The New York Yankees sign Bernie to a minor-league contract.

1986 • Bernie joins the Sarasota Yankees and becomes the top baserunner in the Gulf Coast League.

1988 • Bernie wins the Carolina League batting championship.

1991 • Bernie joins the Yankees after Roberto Kelly injures his wrist. Bernie plays so well that the Yankees make him their center fielder.

1994 • Bernie's best season ends early when the players strike in August.

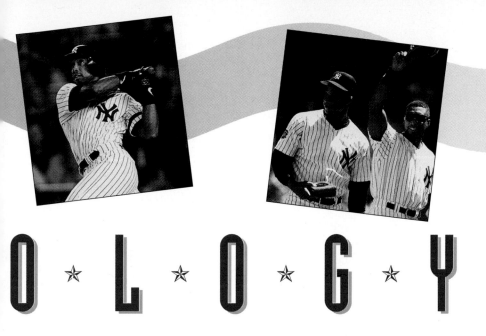

O ⋆ L ⋆ O ⋆ G ⋆ Y

1995
- The Yankees win the American League wild card, but lose to the Seattle Mariners in a tough series. Bernie plays magnificently, batting .429 with eight runs scored.

1996
- The Yankees seize first place and win the division. Bernie plays brilliant defense and offense in the playoffs, leading the Yankees past both the Texas Rangers and the Baltimore Orioles. He is voted MVP of the American League Championship Series. The Yankees go on to win the World Series.

1997
- The Yankees win the American League wild card, but are eliminated by the Cleveland Indians.